TERRORIST ATTACKS

MURDER AT THE 1972 OLYMPICS IN MUNICH

Liz Sonneborn

The Rosen Publishing Group, Inc.
New York

Published in 2003 by The Rosen Publishing Group, Inc.
29 East 21st Street, New York, NY 10010

Library of Congress Cataloging-in-Publication Data

Sonneborn, Liz.
Murder at the 1972 Olympics in Munich / by Liz Sonneborn. — 1st ed.
p. cm. — (Terrorist attacks)
Includes bibliographical references and index.
ISBN 0-8239-3654-6 (lib. bdg.)
1. Terrorism—Germany—Munich. 2. Athletes—Violence against—Germany—Munich. 3. Israelis—Violence against—Germany—Munich. 4. Olympic Games (20th: 1972: Munich, Germany). 5. Munaòzòzamat Aylåul al-Aswad. I. Title. II. Series.
HV6433.G32 M857 2003
364.15'23'0943364—dc21

2001006637

Manufactured in the United States of America

CONTENTS

INTRODUCTION

In the summer of 1972, more than 10,000 athletes from around the globe flooded into Munich, a city in the southern region of what was then West Germany. They came for the twentieth summer Olympic Games. Nearly every four years since 1896, the Olympics had brought together the world's greatest amateur athletes to compete against one another. Delighted to host the international event, the Germans declared that the Munich Olympics would be the "Games of Peace and Joy."

West Germany had a good deal riding on the Munich Olympics. It hoped to erase the public's memory of the last time Germany had hosted the games. The year was 1936, and German dictator Adolf Hitler had recently risen to power. Hitler tried to use the Olympics, held in the city of Berlin, to showcase his belief that Aryans—non–Jewish whites—were a superior people. Despite his efforts, the star of the 1936 Olympics was Jesse Owens, an African American athlete who won four gold medals. To Hitler's irritation, Owens's incredible performance single-handedly discredited the dictator's racist views.

Only three years after the Berlin Olympics, Hitler's desire to rule all of Europe sparked World War II (1939–1945). After Hitler was defeated, Germany was divided into two countries. East Germany was a communist state, while West Germany was a democracy. For the next thirty years, West Germany struggled to put the past behind it. But because of Hitler's deeds, many people still distrusted Germans.

Officials in West Germany saw the Olympics as the perfect vehicle to change people's minds. By hosting the games, they wanted to show the world that West Germany was a free and modern country, full of warm and friendly people. For ten days, the Munich Olympics lived up to their greatest expectations. The games went smoothly and showed West Germany at its best. Spectators and a huge television audience were thrilled by the performances of the athletes.

The events of September 5, the eleventh day of the games, changed everything. Today, the triumphs of most of the athletes at Munich are long forgotten. But the tragedy of that day remains fresh. It was then that the Olympics became the stage for one of the most savage terrorist attacks of the twentieth century. As a result, the Munich Games are now remembered not as the Olympics of peace and joy, but as the Olympics of terror and murder.

The 1972 Olympics in Munich were the first to be held in Germany since the Berlin Olympics, held in 1936 under Adolf Hitler's rule.

BLACK SEPTEMBER

On August 26, 1972, a television audience of one billion watched the opening ceremonies of the Munich Olympics. One by one, the teams from each participating country marched into Olympic Stadium as the crowd cheered. The moment was emotional for every athlete. They had worked for years, perhaps for their entire lives, for a chance to compete in the Olympics.

The opening of the games had a special significance for one team—the team from Israel. Each of the team members was Jewish, as are the majority of Israelis. Some thirty years earlier, many of the athletes' families had been victims of German dictator Adolf Hitler, who had tried to destroy the Jewish people. During World War II, his followers, the Nazis, murdered more than six million Jews.

The organizers of the Munich Olympics worked hard to keep from reminding the world of what the Nazis had done. The organizers even refused to let security guards carry weapons, for fear of evoking memories of heavily armed Nazi soldiers. In an interview for the documentary *One Day in September,* Shmuel Lalkin, the head of the Israeli delegation, later recalled, "the atmosphere was . . . enjoy yourself, see that Germany is not the same as it was."

Still, many of the Israelis felt nervous on German soil. Weight lifting trainer Tuvia Sokolovsky had lost most of his family during the war. Quoted in Peter Taylor's book *States of Terror,* he explained the tension he felt in Munich: "I had a horrible feeling as I saw in every adult German the face of the murderers of my parents." Henry Herskowitz, who participated in the rifle shooting competition, later said in an interview for *One Day in September* that he "had a feeling that something might happen." After he was chosen to carry Israel's flag in the opening ceremonies, he worried he could become the target of a German assassin.

The Olympic Ideal

Fortunately, Herskowitz's fear was unfounded. In the first days of the games, the Israeli athletes were treated like any others. Their presence seemed to confirm what was

Smoke pours from a building in Jerusalem after an attack by Palestinian terrorists. These terrorists target people not just in the Middle East, but around the world.

special about the Olympics. At the games, athletes from different countries—even countries that were enemies of one another—could put aside their differences. If for only a few days every four years, the Olympics allowed people from all nations to come together in peace.

Despite the friendly atmosphere, as the games were winding down, the Israelis were looking forward to leaving Munich and heading home. On September 4, many of the Israeli athletes decided to have one last night out. They took in a local production of *Fiddler on the Roof* and then headed back to their rooms at Olympic Village for a good night's sleep before the games resumed the next morning.

Palestine and Israel

While the Israelis were enjoying a night on the town, ten Palestinians met at a restaurant in the Munich railway station. They were members of the terrorist group Black September. For two years, Black September had been committing acts of terrorism, such as planting bombs and killing leaders. Its goal was to focus the world's attention on the Arabs in Palestine.

Roughly the area between the Jordan River and the Mediterranean Sea, Palestine had once been part of the ancient kingdom of Israel. It had been ruled by the Jewish king David beginning in about 1000 BC. The kingdom, however, was later taken over by the Romans. By about AD 100, Jews were violently expelled from the region. They were left to wander through Europe, without a homeland of their own.

THE BATTLE OF BLACK SEPTEMBER

The Black September terrorist group took its name from one of the bloodiest battles ever fought by the Palestinians. By the late 1960s, Palestinian guerrillas were launching regular terrorist attacks on the people of Israel. Arab fighters set up large bases in the nearby Arab country of Jordan. Jordan's leader, King Hussein, soon became concerned by the Palestinians' growing numbers and strength. At the urging of his army chiefs, he ordered Jordanian soldiers to drive them out of his country. On the morning of September 17, 1970, the army's tanks rolled toward the guerrilla camps. By the end of the battle—later nicknamed Black September—more than 4,000 Palestinian guerrillas had died.

In the seventh century, Arabs emerged as a powerful force in Palestine. They were mostly Muslims, people who practice the religion of Islam. Arabs controlled the area until after World War I, when Palestine came under British rule. By that time, many Jews had become supporters of Zionism. Zionists wanted to establish a new Jewish homeland in Palestine. Many Jews started moving to Palestine in the hope that one day it would again be the home to their people.

The Arab Palestinians were angry about these Jewish immigrants. They feared that the newcomers wanted to take over the land. Fighting often broke out between Arabs and Jews. The violence grew worse after 1948, when the United Nations recognized the state of Israel as a separate and independent nation. This new country included territory the Palestinians thought of as their own.

After the formation of Israel, about 700,000 Palestinians left their homes in fear for their lives. Overwhelmed by Israeli soldiers, hundreds of thousands more were forced into crowded refugee camps. The refugees survived on food rations. They lived in tin huts that did little to protect them from the scorching summer heat or harsh winter winds.

Many young men in the camps vowed that one day they would liberate Palestine from their Israeli enemies. One of them was Jamal Al Gashey. In his teens, he joined the terrorist group Fatah. In an interview for the documentary *One Day in September*, he later explained the sense of fulfillment

This plane was blown apart by a bomb, and is but one example of the destruction that has been wrought by Palestinian terrorists.

he felt when he held a gun during his Fatah training: "For the first time, I felt proud and felt that my existence and my life had a meaning, that I was not just a wretched refugee, but a revolutionary fighting for a cause."

The Terrorists' Mission

In the summer of 1972, Al Gashey was chosen for a special mission of Black September, an offshoot of Fatah. He spent a month in Libya, training for the secret operation. In early September, he was sent to Munich. Al Gashey spent a few days enjoying the Olympics, attending a few volleyball games while waiting to hear more about the operation.

Sitting with seven other terrorists at the Munich railway station, Al Gashey learned what his mission would be. Two Black September leaders instructed the terrorists to take as many Israeli athletes as possible hostage. The eight men were then given a list of Palestinians held in Israeli prisons. They were supposed to negotiate a trade: They would release the athletes only after Israel released all of the prisoners on the list. Although Al Gashey was just nineteen, he felt no fear as the terrorists headed for Olympic Village in the early hours of September 5. Instead, he later recalled, "Personally, I felt pride and joy. My dream of taking part in an operation against the Israelis was coming true."

Athletes from around the world march through Munich's Olympic Stadium during the opening ceremonies of the 1972 Games.

ASSAULT ON 31 CONNOLLYSTRASSE

![chapter banner]

CHAPTER 2

At about 4:00 AM, the Black September terrorists arrived at Olympic Village. Their leader, Luttif "Issa" Afif, knew just what to do. He and his second-in-command, Yusuf "Tony" Nazzal, had spent days staking out the area. Just the night before, they had sneaked into 31 Connollystrasse to have a look around. In the building were six apartments, in which their targets—the twenty-one members of Israel's team—were staying.

Before the terrorists could reach the building, they had to scale a six-foot fence that surrounded Olympic Village. Afif and Nazzal's preparations proved useful. They had watched several athletes sneak into

31 Connollystrasse is the building in which the Black September terrorists held their Israeli hostages.

the village late at night over a certain length of fence. There were few security guards in the area, making it easy to get inside unnoticed. Just in case a guard came along, they all wore tracksuits to make them look like athletes. They also carried gym bags stuffed with grenades and rifles. After hopping the fence, the terrorists headed off to begin their deadly mission.

Afif knew that the Israelis at 31 Connollystrasse were staying in apartments 1 through 6. When he and the other terrorists reached the building, they tried the outside door to apartment 1. It had been left unlocked. Afif pulled out a key he had obtained earlier to open the inside door.

Inside apartment 1 were seven Israelis, asleep in several bedrooms surrounding a central lounge. Hearing the rustling outside, Yossef Gutfreund, a wrestling referee, woke up. Slowly, he stumbled out of his bedroom into the lounge, just as the door began to open. Immediately, he spied the terrorists' guns. Gutfreund shouted out in terror, crying for the others in the apartment to take cover. At the same time, he threw his nearly 300-pound body against the door, as three of the terrorists struggled to push it open.

Tuvia Sokolovsky, a weight lifting trainer who was sharing Gutfreund's room, rushed into the lounge. He screamed to awaken his friends, then ran back to the bedroom. In his panic, he managed to open a window and slip outside. By that time, the terrorists had pushed past Gutfreund and raced into his bedroom. They opened fire on Sokolovsky as he ran down the street in his pajamas. He later remembered hearing bullets flying, but he was able to escape unharmed.

Taking Hostages

In the apartment, the terrorists began rounding up the Israelis in the other bedrooms. As Afif burst into one bedroom, he was attacked by wrestling coach Moshe Weinberg. Weinberg had only a fruit knife to defend himself, but he was able to slice Afif's jacket. Another terrorist leveled his gun at Weinberg's head and fired. A bullet struck Weinberg in the mouth, splattering the room with blood.

The terrorists tied the wrists and ankles of the five other Israelis that they managed to take hostage. In addition to Gutfreund, they were coaches Amitzur Shapira, Kehat Shorr, and Andre Spitzer, and weight lifting judge Jacov Springer. Afif and two other terrorists held their rifles on the hostages, while Nazzal and the other four of his men dragged the wounded Weinberg onto the street. They headed toward apartment 3, where six Israeli wrestlers and weight lifters lay sleeping.

Seven of the murdered Israeli athletes. From left to right: *(top)* Yossef Romano, Amitzur Shapira, David Berger; *(middle)* Andre Spitzer, Mark Slavin, Zeev Friedman; *(bottom)* Kehat Shorr.

Inside apartment 3, the terrorists first captured Mark Slavin and Eliezer Halfin. Hearing the noise, Gad Tsabari and David Berger came out of their rooms to find a Palestinian terrorist holding a gun on their friends. All four were herded outside, where they saw that the two other athletes in the apartment, Yossef Romano and Zeev Friedman, had also been taken captive. With them was the barely conscious Weinberg, his mouth still bleeding heavily. Speaking in Hebrew, Berger urged his fellow hostages, "Let's pounce on them! We have nothing to lose." Unfortunately for the Israelis, one of the terrorists understood Hebrew. He pointed his gun menacingly to dissuade the athletes from trying to overpower their captors.

Tsabari, however, could not shake Berger's words. As the Palestinian terrorists forced the Israelis to walk to apartment 1, he decided that with nothing to lose, he might as well try to escape. Tsabari suddenly veered to the side and raced toward a flight of stairs leading to a parking lot. A terrorist followed him shooting, but Tsabari somehow dodged the bullets. "It only lasted a few minutes," he later recalled in a filmed interview, "but every minute was as long as the years of my life."

At the same time, Weinberg again tried to resist the terrorists. He punched one of them and reached for his gun. Before Weinberg could get a hold on it, another terrorist shot him, blowing a hole into his chest.

The terrorists quickly hustled the other hostages into apartment 1. Yossef Romano then made his own attempt to save himself and his friends. As he lunged at a terrorist, one of the Palestinian gunmen tore his body apart with a hail of bullets. Slavin, Halfin, Berger, and Friedman were then tied up and seated with the other five hostages. The terrorists left Romano's bloody corpse in the room as a reminder of what would happen to them if they tried to resist.

This famous image shows a Black September terrorist on the balcony of 31 Connollystrasse during the hostage crisis at the 1972 Olympics.

Making Demands

The Palestinian terrorists considered searching for more hostages, but their shots had alerted the other Israeli athletes in the building. Several other athletes in apartment 2 were already frantically crawling out the back windows. The terrorists decided not to pursue them, satisfied with the nine Israelis they had managed to kidnap.

The gunfire was also heard by a German cleaning lady, who called a security officer. The unarmed policeman strolled down Connollystrasse to find a terrorist holding a gun in the doorway of number 31. Though frightened, the officer yelled out to the gunman, asking what was going on. The terrorist ignored the policeman, who then used his walkie-talkie to alert his force. By about 5:00 AM, Manfred Schreiber, chief of the Munich police, was awakened with the news of the crisis unfolding at Olympic Village.

Ten minutes later, a police officer sent by Schreiber approached 31 Connollystrasse. He held his hands in the air to assure the terrorists he was unarmed. From a second-story window, one of the terrorists dropped two sheets of paper to the officer waiting below. On the sheets were Black September's demands. They would free the hostages only if 236 imprisoned Palestinian terrorists were released. Aside from two in German prisons, all of these prisoners were held in Israeli jails. The deadline for their demands to be met was 9:00 AM.

Palestinian terrorist Luttif "Issa" Afif, his face blackened with shoe polish, talks to Bruno Merck, the Bavarian Minister of the Interior, during the hostage crisis.

The German authorities hoped they could negotiate with the terrorists. But their demands offered little hope. Israel's leader, Prime Minister Golda Meir, had always refused to bow to terrorists. It seemed highly unlikely that she would change her policy now, especially considering how many prisoners the terrorists wanted released.

As the Germans sent word to Israel, the police worked to keep the lines of communication open. They sent Annaliese Graes, a forty-one-year-old policewoman, to 31 Connollystrasse to talk with the terrorists. As she approached the building, Afif emerged. He wore a linen suit, his face blackened with shoe polish.

Graes immediately challenged Afif. She asked him why he had made demands that Germany could not possibly meet. Only Israel could agree to free most of the prisoners he had named. Afif told her Black September had no trouble with Germany, but his demands were set. According to testimony Graes later gave to a Bavarian government investigator, Afif said, "Free all those prisoners or all the hostages will die."

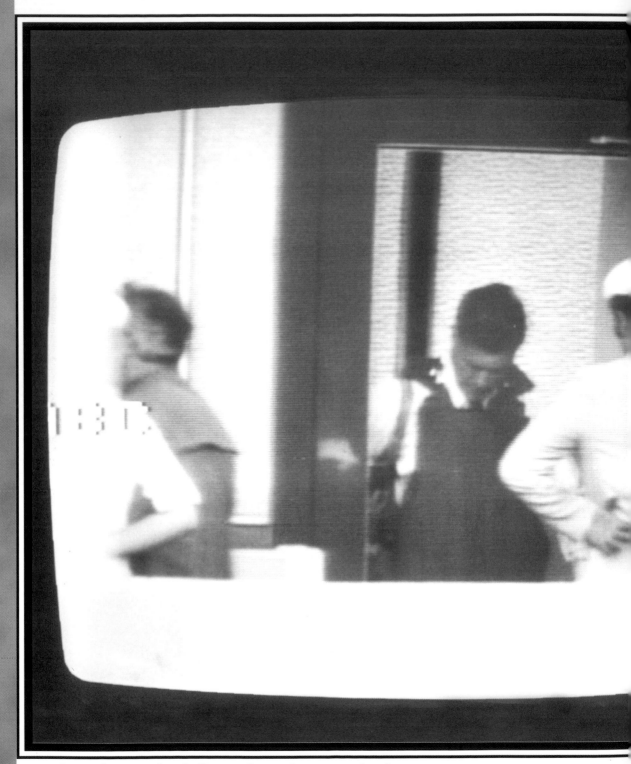

Police volunteers don bulletproof vests in preparation for storming 31 Connollystrasse.

NEGOTIATING A RELEASE

As the German authorities tried to figure out how to handle the hostage crisis, one thing became clear: They could not possibly meet the 9:00 AM deadline set by the terrorists. At about 8:45 AM, Munich police chief Manfred Schreiber cautiously approached 31 Connollystrasse. He was accompanied by Walther Tröger, mayor of Olympic Village, and A. D. Touny, an Egyptian member of the International Olympic Committee. The Germans thought the terrorists might be more willing to talk to Touny, who, like them, was an Arab.

Afif emerged from the building to meet with the three negotiators. He repeated his demands, making it clear that they were not open to discussion. To the negotiators' relief, however, Afif immediately agreed to extend the deadline to 12:00 PM. During the tense meeting, Schreiber considered grabbing Afif and taking him hostage. But, sensing what Schreiber was thinking, Afif held out his hand, showing that his finger was on the pin of a grenade. Afif told Schreiber that if he tried anything, he would blow them both up.

The Germans now had three more hours to come up with a solution to the crisis. In the West German capital of Bonn, Chancellor Willy Brandt authorized the negotiators to pay any amount of money to secure the hostages' release. Several German officials also offered to take the Israelis' place and become hostages themselves.

Neither offer interested Afif. He stuck to the demands his Black September superiors had set, even as Tröger tried to convince him that their actions would hurt the Palestinian cause. Afif disagreed. He was convinced their terrorist act would bring needed attention to the Palestinians' plight. Tröger stated in the documentary, *One Day in September*, that Afif said, "We are dead anyway, either we will be killed here, or if we go out and give up without having hostages . . . we will be killed where[ever] we go." To Tröger, Afif seemed to be saying that if the terrorists abandoned their mission, they would be branded as cowards and killed by other Palestinians.

Throughout her tenure as Israeli prime minister, Golda Meir refused to be intimidated by Palestinian terrorists.

While the negotiations continued, the families of the Israeli athletes woke to the news that their loved ones might be in danger. Prime Minister Golda Meir confirmed the worst fears of the hostages' relatives in a ten-minute address to Israel's parliament. After reading the names of the nine hostages, she confirmed that the terrorists had threatened to kill them all.

As the Germans had expected, Meir refused to consider dealing with the terrorists. She said if she gave in to them, no Israeli anywhere in the world could ever feel safe again. Meir sent word that the Germans could handle the crisis as they wished. But under no circumstances would she release any prisoners. The Germans kept the information from Afif, who still seemed hopeful that Israel would meet his demands.

The Games Continue

Adding to the pressure on the German authorities were the demands of Avery Brundage, the American head of the International Olympic Committee. He wanted an end to the standoff with the terrorists because it was casting a pall over the Olympics. Despite the hostage crisis, Brundage stubbornly refused to suspend the morning games.

Television coverage cut back and forth between the competitions and the life-and-death situation at 31 Connollystrasse. Many viewers were disgusted at seeing images of cheering crowds intercut with shots of the Palestinian terrorists. Several television commentators even seemed offended by the fact that events were continuing. Finally, Brundage reluctantly agreed to suspend the afternoon's games. He also scheduled a memorial at Olympic Stadium for Moshe Weinberg and Yossef Romano, the two Israelis who had been killed, for the next morning at 10:00 AM.

As news spread about the unfolding hostage situation, journalists and film crews flocked to Olympic Village. Many staked out balconies of buildings overlooking 31 Connollystrasse. There, they could keep their cameras focused on the building's blue door. Every once in a while, they caught on film one of the armed Arab terrorists peering at the scene outside.

In the United States and many other countries, the crisis was covered by the ABC television network, with sports journalist Jim McKay serving as anchor. Live reports were provided by Peter Jennings, a reporter usually stationed in the Middle East who happened to be covering the Olympics. From a building across the street from 31 Connollystrasse, Jennings gave a running commentary into a walkie-talkie that was instantly broadcast throughout much of the world.

Hoping to see what was happening for themselves, thousands of spectators also crowded into Olympic Village. Their curiosity lent a circuslike air to the crisis that unnerved many of the journalists covering the event. In an interview for *One Day in September,* reporter Gerald Seymour said, "There was something unpleasant, selfish, slightly obscene about the atmosphere."

Inside 31 Connollystrasse

As the crowd gathered, the nine Israeli hostages remained tied up, with a guard aiming his gun at them, waiting for any sudden movement. The apartment was splattered with blood. Yossef Romano's corpse, covered with a sheet, still lay in the middle of the room.

The terrified hostages were mostly silent. But terrorist Jamal Al Gashey later recalled that occasionally they tried to engage their captors in conversation. One Israeli even suggested that they share jokes with one another. He began telling a funny story, when Afif walked into the room and told everyone to be quiet. Afif did not want the Palestinians to get too friendly with their captives. He knew that any emotional ties could make it difficult for his men to kill the Israelis if the negotiations soured.

As the 12:00 PM deadline approached, Schreiber, Tröger, and Touny again appeared outside 31 Connollystrasse. They asked Afif for still another extension. Lying, Schreiber told the terrorist leader that Israel could not possibly locate and free all the prisoners he wanted released before noon. In fact, the negotiators just wanted to buy more time to come up with a plan.

Afif was growing weary. He gave them one more hour, hardly enough time for the Germans to figure out a way of resolving the crisis. And this time, he promised that if his demands were not met by the new deadline, he would kill two hostages outside the building for all the news cameras to see. Driving his point home, he held up two fingers. Journalists erroneously reported that he flashed a victory sign, not understanding the more grisly meaning behind the gesture.

An Offer of Help

Desperate for more time, the Germans brought in two high-level officials as negotiators: Hans-Dietrich Genscher, the interior secretary of West Germany, and Bruno Merck, the interior secretary of Bavaria, the German state in which Munich is located. They secured a new deadline of 3:00 PM from Afif, but still the Germans did not know what to do next. They had done all they could to persuade the terrorists to surrender or change their demands, but the Palestinian terrorists stood firm. Any hope for a peaceful resolution to the standoff began to seem unlikely.

At this point, according to Israeli authorities, Israel came up with its own proposal to end the crisis. Meir prepared to fly the Sayeret Matkal to Munich. The Sayeret Matkal were an elite team of Israeli soldiers, one of the only antiterrorist squads in the world trained in hostage rescue. Israeli officials later claimed their offer was refused by West Germany, even though West Germany had no antiterrorist force of its own. Authorities in Bonn apparently decided that a problem on German soil required a German solution.

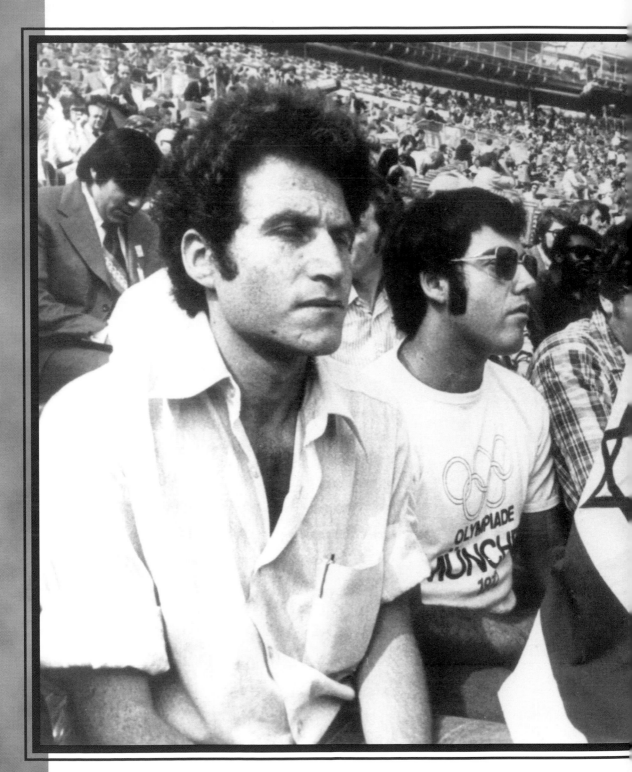

Some 80,000 people attended a memorial service in Olympic Stadium for the eleven Israeli athletes murdered by Palestinian terrorists at the 1972 Games.

PLANNING A RESCUE

B y 2:00 PM, Black September had been holding the Israeli athletes for more than ten hours. The hostages, terrorists, and negotiators were all exhausted. Seeing that the Israelis were hungry as well, Afif ordered the Germans to bring them enough food to feed twenty people. The terrorists, however, would eat none of it. They had brought their own food, fearing that any the Germans gave them might be poisoned.

A Missed Chance

In Afif's request, the German negotiators saw an opportunity. They still did not know exactly how many terrorists there were—a crucial piece of information if they were going to overtake

Manfred Schreiber negotiates an extension with one of the Black September terrorists.

the Palestinians by force. The Germans packed the food in four large boxes, which were carried to the blue door by Schreiber, Tröger, and two police officers who were dressed as chefs.

Schreiber had hoped the terrorists would let them bring the food inside, giving them an opportunity to count the terrorists and scope out the room. But Afif saw through their plan. He had them put the boxes down and carried them into the building himself. Schreiber and the others walked away, with no more information to plan their attack.

As the 3:00 PM deadline approached, the Germans realized they needed still more time. Schreiber, Tröger, Genscher, and Merck returned to 31 Connollystrasse to negotiate another extension. They brought with them Mohammed Khadif, the leader of the Arab League in Bonn.

A cranky Afif was in no mood to hear their request. He became furious and threatened to shoot one of the athletes right then and there. Khadif, though, was able to calm him by saying the murder would only make the Palestinians look like cold-blooded killers.

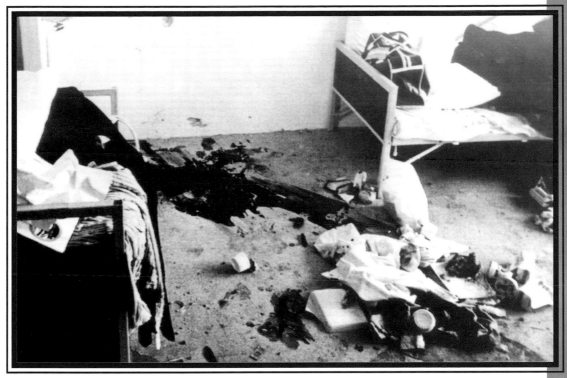

Bloodstains and bullet holes mark the spot where Israeli weight lifter Yossef Romano was murdered by Palestinian terrorists at the apartment at 31 Connollystrasse.

Afif's Plan

Afif hesitantly extended the deadline to 5:00 PM. Predictably, as the hour approached, the German negotiators returned to talk with Afif. This time, he had had enough. Although he tried to act confidently, he sensed that Israel had refused to meet Black September's demands. The Germans were clearly stalling for time, probably because they were trying to organize a rescue mission.

When the German officials asked for an extension, Afif began yelling. According to Serge Groussard's book, *The Blood of Israel*, Afif shouted, "You're not going to trick us! You're not going to play around with us." He was quiet for a moment, then told the Germans to wait and walked back inside.

After a few minutes, he emerged with a plan to end the exhausting standoff. Afif wanted two planes to fly the terrorists and hostages to Cairo, the capital of Egypt. Egypt was an Arab nation that was friendly with the United States and other Western countries. Tired of dealing with the Germans, Afif believed negotiations might go smoother if they were conducted on Arab soil.

The German negotiators tried to talk Afif out of his plan. They knew Israeli officials would be outraged if the terrorists were allowed to take the hostages to an Arab country. The Germans again offered Afif money and brought up the idea of a hostage swap.

Afif had no interest in compromising. He said he would accept one plane instead of two, but otherwise he stayed firm. The Germans then made their own demand. They wanted to see the hostages to make sure they were still alive.

Afif shouted to his men inside, who brought Andre Spitzer, the fencing coach, to a window. Speaking in German, Spitzer confirmed that no one had been killed since the initial attack. But the Germans were still not satisfied. They insisted on seeing the hostages for themselves before making any deals.

Afif finally allowed Genscher and Tröger to come inside. The Germans were horrified by what they saw. All the athletes were seated in one room, their hands tied. Three-hundred-pound Gutfreund was tied to a chair to keep him from making trouble for the terrorists. The room stank of blood and rotting food, and the blood-splattered wall was covered with bullet holes. Genscher later said in an interview for *One Day in September*, "This picture of the room . . . will stay with me as long as I live. I will never forget those faces, full of fear, yet full of hope."

Operation Sunshine

The Germans felt they had no choice but to agree to Afif's demands, although they knew they could not let the terrorists and hostages leave West Germany. The time had come to stage a rescue. The mission was given the name Operation Sunshine. Dozens of German policemen, armed with machine guns and wearing tracksuits and bulletproof vests, were sent onto the roof of 31 Connollystrasse. When they heard the code word Sonnenschein (German for "sunshine"), they were to storm the building through its ventilator shafts and shoot the terrorists.

The operation would be dangerous in the best of conditions. And the conditions were far from good. None of the police involved had any training in dealing with terrorists. The apartment in which the hostages were being held had many rooms and hidden spaces, from which the terrorists could surprise them. Genscher and Tröger had seen five Palestinians, but they had no idea if there were more.

Adding to the operation's difficulties was the crowd of 80,000 that had gathered outside 31 Connollystrasse. While the police tried to sneak onto the roof, the spectators started shouting instructions to them, which alerted the terrorists. The terrorists were certainly warned of the attack by the television

West German police officers armed with machine guns climb onto the roof of 31 Connollystrasse in a failed attempt to free the Israeli hostages.

coverage. Cameras pointed at the building showed the police in place, waiting to enter the building. Like millions of viewers around the globe, the terrorists were watching the operation unfold live on the television inside apartment 1.

Realizing the terrorists were aware of the impending attack, the German police abandoned Operation Sunshine. One policeman involved, Heinz Hohensinn, later remembered his relief at the news during an interview for *One Day in September*: "I am happy and thankful to God that we never got the code word Sonnenschein because if we had I'm not quite sure if I would [be] sit[ting] here today. We saw the whole thing as a suicide mission."

A New Mission

With the failure of Operation Sunshine, the German authorities gave up the idea of storming 31 Connollystrasse. They instead decided to stage a rescue at Fürstenfeldbruck, a small airport near Munich. The Germans would take the terrorists and hostages there, pretending that a plane would then transport them to Cairo. When the terrorists were in the open space of the runway, German snipers would be able to gun them down.

As the Germans planned the trip to the airport, they came up with another idea. They decided to transport the terrorists and hostages to Fürstenfeldbruck by helicopter. To reach the helicopters, the terrorists would have to walk 180 yards through a parking garage underneath the Olympic Village buildings. The police decided to position snipers inside to pick off the Palestinians as they made their way through the garage.

When the negotiators told Afif how they would reach the airport, he again suspected a plot. He insisted on seeing the garage for himself. Telling his men to kill the hostages if he did not return in six minutes, Afif left the building and walked downstairs, accompanied by German officials. There, Afif probably spotted one of several policemen who were already hiding in the garage. He then demanded a bus to transport his men and the Israelis to the waiting helicopters. Their plan discovered, the Germans made a new decision. The assault would have to take place at Fürstenfeldbruck.

Top: The bus carrying the Palestinian terrorists and their Israeli captives leaves to meet the helicopters.

Bottom: People around the world watched a police helicopter transport the hostages and their captors to the airport on broadcast television.

MASSACRE AT THE AIRPORT

At about 10:00 PM, a green bus arrived outside 31 Connollystrasse, ready to take the terrorists and their hostages to the airport. Visibly nervous, the Palestinian terrorists slowly led the blindfolded captives toward the bus in groups of three. Each terrorist pointed his gun into the shadows, fearing an ambush. For the crowd, the moment offered the first chance to see both the Israelis and their captors. The dark sky lit up from the flashes of cameras used by bystanders, who captured morbid souvenirs of the event.

In the bus, the Israelis and Palestinians were taken to two helicopters. The German government had decided not to allow the media to report from the airport. The helicopters rising into the air, therefore, were the last image of the operation shown live on television.

Botched Preparations

While the helicopters headed for Fürstenfeldbruck airport, the German police prepared for their attack. They had assembled only five snipers, based on the reports of the negotiators that they had seen five terrorists. But as the terrorists boarded the bus, it became obvious to everyone watching that there were in fact eight terrorists. Inconceivably, this information was never passed on to the police at Fürstenfeldbruck so they could round up additional snipers.

Three gunmen were positioned on the roof of the airport's central building. Two more were on the ground—one hiding behind a truck, another crouched behind a low stone wall. All soon realized that no one had bothered to set up flood lights. Without the lights, the snipers could hardly see the area where the helicopters were to land.

The snipers on the roof also had not been told the exact location of the others. Getting into position, the sniper behind the wall was horrified to discover that he was in their direct line of fire. He could not communicate the problem because the snipers had not been issued walkie-talkies. The police had also neglected to give them bulletproof vests or steel helmets.

According to the police's plan, as soon as the helicopters landed, Afif and Nazzal would be led to a 727 jet waiting on the runway. While the terrorists were inspecting the plane, eighteen heavily armed police officers hiding in the jet would capture or kill them. The five snipers would then shoot the remaining terrorists, and the hostages would be saved.

The police team on the 727, however, was terrified when they saw the plane. In the small area inside, no one would be safe if a firefight erupted. They were also afraid the terrorists would sense the plot as soon as they came aboard and throw a grenade into the plane, blowing them all to bits. The policemen were even more upset when they learned the plane was full of fuel. If guns were fired on board, they were sure the entire plane would explode. Convinced they were on a suicide mission, the policemen took a vote. Just minutes before the helicopters arrived, they unanimously decided to abandon their posts.

The Helicopters Arrive

The stage was set for disaster as the two helicopters landed. As planned, Afif and Nazzal got out and headed toward the jet. At the same time, the four Germans who had flown the helicopters began to walk away. In earlier negotiations, the Palestinians had agreed to let the pilots go. Instead, they pointed their guns at the Germans, taking all four captive.

Immediately after boarding the crewless jet, Afif and Nazzal knew they were in trouble. They ran off the plane and raced toward the helicopters, yelling to their comrades. By this time, four of the other terrorists were standing outside the helicopters, while two remained inside. Also inside were the hostages, tied up and unable to move.

As Afif and Nazzal shouted, the three snipers on the roof were given orders to open fire. Two of the terrorists were shot, one fatally. The four German pilots ran off in a panic. Nazzal was hit in his leg, while the other terrorists ran for cover under one of the helicopters.

Immediately, the terrorists began returning gunfire. With their machine guns, they fired at the airport buildings, narrowly missing several of the German officials overseeing the operation. They killed one German policeman in the airport's control tower. In the meantime, another terrorist was shot in the chest, while Jamal Al Gashey took a bullet in the hand. The sniper behind the wall nearly shot a man running toward him, but at the last minute recognized him as one of the panicked German pilots.

The gun battle had become a complete free-for-all. None of the German officials knew what to do. Two Israeli officials who had insisted on witnessing the rescue attempt begged to talk to the terrorists. They took a megaphone to the roof and demanded that the Palestinians stop firing. The terrorists responded with a hail of machine gunfire. The Israeli negotiators had to drop to the ground to avoid being hit.

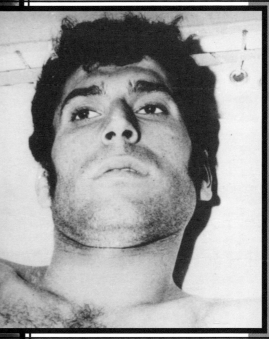

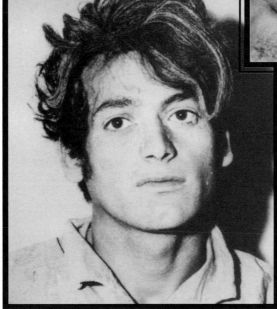

These are three of the Palestinian terrorists who murdered the Israeli Olympic athletes. From top to bottom, they are Sirimer Mohammed Abdullah, Ibrahim Mosoud Badran, and Abed Kair Al Dnawly.

The German officials decided their only hope was to hold off the terrorists until armored cars could arrive at the scene. Unfortunately, no one had thought to request the cars until 10:40 PM, about ten minutes after the firefight had already begun. Unknown to the anxious Germans, the armored cars were stuck in traffic. So many sightseers were trying to get to the airport that the highways leading there were completely jammed.

"Good" News

A huge crowd of onlookers had already gathered outside Fürstenfeldbruck's gates. Many were members of the press. Others were everyday people—even some families with children—caught up in the drama of the event. All were eager to hear what was going on inside the airport gates.

From the crowd, a man wearing an official Olympic hat came forward. For reasons unknown, he announced that all the hostages had been saved. News of the supposed rescue spread fast. At 11:31 PM, the Reuters news agency wired a report throughout the world declaring the crisis was over. German chancellor Willy Brandt's press secretary went on West German television to say all was fine, while Israeli Prime Minister Golda Meir drank a toast with her closest advisers. ABC's Jim McKay confidently predicted that, since all the hostages were reportedly alive, the whole incident would "be forgotten after a few weeks."

One of the helicopters was destroyed by a hand grenade set off by a Palestinian terrorist, killing the sole surviving Israeli Olympic athlete inside.

Slaughter on the Runway

Unknown to the world, the situation at Fürstenfeldbruck was only growing more desperate. At 11:55 PM, four armored cars finally arrived. They positioned themselves on the runway and slowly began heading toward the helicopters.

The terrorists hiding under the helicopters assumed that they would be killed in a hail of gunfire. Before he could be shot down, one terrorist ran into one of the two helicopters and opened fire. Three hostages sitting inside—Jacov Springer, Eliezer Halfin, and Zeev Friedman—were killed instantly. The fourth, David Berger, was—amazingly—only wounded in the leg. But he, too, met his death when the Palestinian terrorist threw a live grenade into the helicopter.

People all over the world grieved for the slain Israeli Olympic athletes.

Just as the helicopter exploded, Afif fired a barrage of bullets toward the airport buildings. He and the murderer of the four Israel athletes were shot dead by the German snipers. Another terrorist, Adnan Al Gashey, slipped into the other helicopter. He fired his machine gun on the five remaining hostages—Yossef Gutfreund, Kehat Shorr, Mark Slavin, Andre Spitzer, and Amitzur Shapira—killing them all.

Even with the hostages dead, the shooting continued. The sniper behind the wall managed to kill another terrorist. But the shooting drew the attention of the police in one of the armored cars. Mistaking the sniper for a terrorist, the police opened fire. The sniper was shot in the buttocks, while a German pilot hiding behind the wall with him was more seriously injured by a bullet in his lung.

Still another terrorist was killed before the shooting finally stopped at about 12:30 AM. The bloodbath had lasted two hours. Of the eight terrorists, three—Jamal Al Gashey,

Adnan Al Gashey, and Mohammed Safady—were still alive and taken into custody by the German police. All four of the German pilots had survived. But all nine of the Israelis were dead, either from bullets or fire.

The World Learns the News

While the Israeli hostages were being slaughtered, the world had been celebrating their release. But by 1:30 AM on the morning of September 6, the media was discovering the true story of what had happened at Fürstenfeldbruck. Jim McKay of ABC told his anxious audience, "There is a report of a burning helicopter. All seems to be confusion. Nothing is nailed down."

An hour and a half later, sadly all confusion was gone. McKay announced, "Our worst fears have been realized tonight," then he explained that all of the hostages were dead. Clearly exhausted, the newsman mournfully asked questions everyone was asking but no one could answer: "What will happen to the Games of the twentieth Olympiad? None of us knows . . . What will happen to the course of world history? . . . I have nothing else to say."

The body of Olympic athlete David Berger is returned to Cleveland, Ohio, for burial.

AFTER THE DISASTER

As scheduled, a memorial was held at Olympic Stadium on the morning of September 6. But it was no longer just for Moshe Weinberg and Yossef Romano, the two athletes murdered during the initial attack on the Israeli team. It was now for all eleven athletes left dead at the hands of Black September.

Not wanting the memorial to be the world's final memory of the Munich Olympics, organizer Avery Brundage pushed for the games to continue. The Olympic athletes were split over the decision. Some were appalled, feeling that continuing the competitions was an insult to the murdered Israelis. Others felt that by abandoning the games, they would be giving in to the terrorists.

Mourning the Dead

Soon after the memorial, the remains of the slain athletes were flown out of Munich. David Berger's body was sent to the United States, where his family lived. The bodies of the other ten were returned to Israel. Nearly 5,000 mourners arrived at Lod Airport in central Israel to meet the coffins and pay their respects to the victims' families.

The five Palestinian terrorists killed during the operation were also mourned in their homeland. During a funeral ceremony in Libya, more than 30,000 people turned out to honor the dead. To the horror of all Israelis, the Black September terrorists who had died emerged as heroes in the Arab world. They were viewed by other Arabs as martyrs in the fight for Palestinian independence.

The Terrorists Go Free

Remaining in Munich were Jamal Al Gashey, Adnan Al Gashey, and Mohammed Safady, the three surviving terrorists. When they were first captured, they had expected to be executed on the spot. To their relief, they were taken into custody, questioned, and placed in prison to await trial. Sitting behind bars, they no doubt wondered whether their Black September comrades were making a plan to secure their freedom.

They did not have to wait long. On October 29, 1972, two Palestinian terrorists hijacked a plane operated by the German airline Lufthansa. They insisted that the airplane, bound for the German city of Frankfurt, be rerouted to Munich.

THE TERRORISTS' LAST WORDS

After the Munich massacre, radio announcers on the Voice of Palestine read a letter that contained the following excerpt. They claimed it was sent to them by the Black September terrorists. Many Israelis, though, held that the letter was written after the terrorists' deaths as a desperate bid to win sympathy for them and their cause.

"We are neither killers nor bandits. We are persecuted people who have no land and no homeland . . . We will the youth of the Arab nation to search for death so that life is given to them, their countries, and their people. Each drop of blood spilled from you and from us will be oil to kindle this nation with flames of victory and liberation."

The hijackers said they would blow up the plane and its eleven passengers unless the German government released the three Munich Olympic terrorists. Claiming that he wanted to "avoid further senseless bloodshed," German chancellor Willy Brandt immediately agreed to their demands. The terrorists were soon returned home to a heroes' welcome.

Several Palestinians have since claimed that the hijacking was a plot hatched by both Black September and the German government. They claim that Black September threatened to commit a rash of terrorist acts in West Germany unless the government let the terrorists go. The Lufthansa hijacking was allegedly staged by German officials to provide an excuse for the terrorists' release. German authorities, however, still dispute these charges.

Operation Wrath of God

Whether or not the Germans masterminded the Lufthansa hijacking, officials in Israel were furious at the Germans for releasing the terrorists. Anger among Israelis over the Munich massacre had already reached a fever pitch. Israel's army had attacked several areas thought to be terrorist strongholds. On September 8, in just one operation, Israel's air force bombed ten camps in Syria and Lebanon, killing about 200 people.

After Germany freed the three Munich terrorists, the Israelis' desire for justice reached new heights. The government decided to do anything it could to stop Black September. Organizing a team of special agents, it launched a secret war against the group, later known as Operation Wrath of God. Its organizer, General Aharon Yariv, explained, "We had to make them stop, and there was no other way . . . We went back to the old biblical rule of an eye for an eye."

Several dozen members of Black September were targeted by the operation. Some received calls that threatened their lives and those of their families. Others were the subjects of fake obituaries that Israeli agents placed in Arab newspapers to frighten terrorists into abandoning their activities. Still others were murdered by Israeli assassins. Among those killed were two of the Munich terrorists—Adnan Al Gashey and Mohammed Safady. The third, Jamal Al Gashey, has so far eluded assassination.

Al Gashey briefly came out of hiding to be interviewed for a 1999 documentary on the Munich Olympic massacre, *One Day in September*. Al Gashey remains proud of his actions in Munich and considers the mission a success because it brought attention to the Palestinians' cause. In the interview, he explained, "Before Munich, the world had no idea about our struggle, but on that day, the name of 'Palestine' was repeated all over the world."

The Search for Truth

Through the years, relatives of the slain Israeli athletes received calls from Israeli agents, telling them of the latest assassinations of Black September members. But many relatives were less interested in revenge than in discovering exactly what happened at Fürstenfeldbruck the night their loved ones died. Among them were Ilana Romano, the wife of murdered athlete Yossef Romano. His death left her a widow at twenty-six, with three small children to raise. As she later explained in an interview for *One Day in September*, "I swore I would find out what happened, for the sake of my daughters."

Equally determined to get to the truth was Ankie Spitzer, who had been married for a year to fencing coach Andre Spitzer until he was killed. She asked German officials for information about the rescue bid. Officials insisted all they had was a sixty-three-page report on the incident, but Spitzer was unconvinced. She suspected the Germans had studied the matter in depth but did not want their findings known.

While struggling to raise their daughter, Ankie Spitzer spent years writing hundreds of letters to officials in Germany and Israel. Again and again, she was told the information she wanted did not exist. But she and other surviving relatives persisted. In an interview for *One Day in September*, Ilana Romano speculated, "Maybe [the Germans] thought these widows [would] go away some day . . . But they forgot that we did not want to let it go because we have a right to know as families what happened to our loved ones."

Hope for Justice

After two decades, Ankie Spitzer finally got what she was looking for. In 1992, after she appeared on German television for a report on the twentieth anniversary of the Munich massacre, she received a call from a German man who refused to identify himself. He promised to sneak the documents she wanted out of German government archives and send them to her.

Two weeks later, Spitzer received a package of documents. It was clear to Spitzer that Germany had made an extensive investigation into the incident. The documents even included an index of more than 3,000 reports investigators had compiled. Armed with this evidence, Spitzer succeeded in forcing Germany to release these materials. They revealed the series of fatal mistakes made by German officials that contributed to the deaths of the Israeli hostages.

The information Spitzer uncovered has become the basis of a lawsuit filed by the murdered athletes' relatives. It

Arab terrorist violence continues to the present day. Now it is directed not only at Jews but at non-Muslims throughout the world.

accuses the German and Bavarian governments of gross mismanagement and misconduct in handling the crisis. After years in the courts, the suit was set aside by the families at the request of the Bavarian government, which agreed to offer a settlement.

In May 2001, the government proposed a total payment of 6 million German marks (about 2.7 million U.S. dollars). The families rejected the settlement, noting that the number was an uncomfortable reminder of the six million Jews murdered by the Germans in the Holocaust during World War II. They instead demanded 11 million marks, 1 million for each of the Israeli athletes murdered. As negotiations continue, the sum remains less important to the relatives than the admission of guilt behind it. As Ankie Spitzer maintains, "I don't want money. I don't want revenge. I just want the truth to be known."

GLOSSARY

Arabs Peoples of the Middle East who speak Arabic.

Aryan A non-Jewish Caucasian, thought by Adolf Hitler to be the master race.

guerrilla A member of an informal military group that attacks its enemies in surprise raids.

hijack To take control of a vehicle, especially an airplane, by force.

martyr A person who chooses to die for a political or religious cause.

Palestine A region in the Middle East including the land between the Mediterranean Sea and the Jordan River.

refugee A person who flees his or her country to escape war or persecution.

sniper A person trained in shooting enemies from a concealed place.

terrorism The use of violence by a person or group to draw attention to their political beliefs or eliminate their enemies.

Zionism A movement dedicated to creating and developing the Jewish state of Israel in Palestine.

For More Information

Museum and Olympic Studies Centre
Villa Olympique
1, Quai d'Ouchy
1006 Lausanne
Switzerland
(41-21) 621-65-11
Web site: http://www.museum.olympic.org

Simon Wiesenthal Center
1399 South Roxbury Drive
Los Angeles, CA 90035
(310) 553-9036
(800) 900-9036
e-mail: information@wiesenthal.net
Web site: http://www.wiesenthal.com

United States Olympic Committee
National Headquarters
One Olympic Plaza
Colorado Springs, CO 80909
(719) 632-5551
e-mail: media@usoc.org
Web site: http://www.usolympicteam.com

Video

One Day in September. Culver City, CA: Columbia Tristar
Home Video, 2001.

Web Sites

Due to the changing nature of Internet links, the Rosen
Publishing Group, Inc., has developed an online list of
Web sites related to the subject of this book. This site is
updated regularly. Please use this link to access the list:

http://www.rosenlinks.com/tat/mnom/

FOR FURTHER READING

Anderson, Dave. *The Story of the Olympics.* Rev. ed. New York: HarperCollins, 2000.

Long, Cathryn J. *The Middle East in Search of Peace.* Brookfield, CT: Millbrook Press, 1996.

Marcovitz, Hal. *Terrorism.* Philadelphia, PA: Chelsea House Publishers, 2000.

Middleton, Haydn. *Crises at the Olympics.* Des Plaines, IL: Heinemann Library, 2000.

Ross, Stewart. *Causes and Consequences of the Arab-Israeli Conflict.* Austin, TX: Raintree/ Steck-Vaughn, 1995.

BIBLIOGRAPHY

Battsek, John, and Arthur Cohn, prods. *One Day in September*. Culver City, CA: Columbia Tristar Home Video, 2001.

Coote, James, and John Goodbody. *The Olympics 1972*. London: Hale, 1972.

Reeve, Simon. *One Day in September.* New York: Arcade Publishing, 2000.

Sandomir, Richard. "When Innocence Died at the Olympics." *The New York Times.* September 3, 2000.

Schaffer, Kay, and Sidonie Smith, eds. *The Olympics at the Millennium: Power, Politics, and the Games.* New Brunswick, NJ: Rutgers University Press, 2000.

" '6M Marks' Offer Upsets Munich Victims' Families." *USA Today*. May 2, 2001.

Von Drehle, David. "More Than a Game." *The Washington Post*. September 2, 2000.

INDEX

About the Author

Liz Sonneborn is a writer and an editor who lives in Brooklyn, New York. A graduate of Swarthmore College, she has written more than twenty books for children and adults, including *A to Z of American Women in the Performing Arts*, *The Scholastic History of the American West*, and *The New York Public Library's Amazing Native American History*, winner of a 2000 Parent's Choice Award.

Photo Credits

Cover © TimePix; cover insets © Hulton/Archive/Getty Images and AP/Wide World Photos; pp. 6–7, 14–15, 20, 22, 45, 48, 57 © Hulton/Archive/Getty Images; pp. 9, 12, 16, 18, 24–25, 32–33, 34, 35, 38, 40 (top and bottom), 47, 50–51 © AP/Wide World Photos; p. 27 © David Rubinger/Corbis.

Editor

Christine Poolos

Series Design and Layout

Geri Giordano